GIVING UP IS NOT AN
OPTION

*One Man's Struggle to Make
the Impossible Possible*

HAZEN MEEK AND LINDA PIERSON MEEK

abbott press

Abbott Press books may be ordered through booksellers or by contacting:

Abbott Press
1663 Liberty Drive
Bloomington, IN 47403
www.abbottpress.com
Phone: 1-866-697-5310

Because of the dynamic nature of the Internet, any web addresses or
links contained in this book may have changed since publication and
may no longer be valid. The views expressed in this work are solely those
of the author and do not necessarily reflect the views of the publisher,
and the publisher hereby disclaims any responsibility for them.

Any people depicted in stock imagery provided by Thinkstock are
models, and such images are being used for illustrative purposes only.
Certain stock imagery © Thinkstock.

ISBN: 978-1-4582-1728-8 (sc)
ISBN: 978-1-4582-1729-5 (e)

Library of Congress Control Number: 2014912947

Printed in the United States of America.

Abbott Press rev. date: 10/02/2014

This book is dedicated to the smartest, funniest,
and strongest man I ever met in my life.
Hazen, this is your book, you did it!!!!

Also, without these dear friends, this book would not
have been possible. I thank Jean Baker Smith, Randy
Smith, and Sharon Fair for their loving support in putting
Hazen's writings together. The help they have all given
me compiling this book, was out of love. We all knew it
was Hazen's wish for this to be published to help others.
Thank you all for "not giving up" on this book. Love linda

PROLOGUE

Written by Linda Pierson Meek

MARCH 15, 2013

As it turned out, while giving my husband a sponge bath, the Hospice nurse said to him, "Hazen, if you're going to pass on, do it while I'm here so your wife will not be alone."

Normally, the Hospice Aid came at 9:00 AM. I was usually dragging myself off the couch next to Hazens's hospital bed after only 3 hours sleep, every day when she arrived. His pain would be so severe that it would keep him awake for hours on end. I was either giving him pain medication, back rubs or providing him with the urinal through the night, so I only managed about 3 hours sleep each night. This particular day she was late. For some unknown reason, Hazen had slept soundly the night before.

I even slept with him in his hospital bed, curled up tightly against him holding his arm against my chest.

Finally, a restful night's sleep! It was 9:00 AM and I was ready to go do a few errands once the Aid arrived to give him his daily sponge bath. I waited and waited. I was getting "antsy." It was now 10:30 AM and the Hospice Aid still had not arrived. I called to find out where she was. The aid called back to tell me she was caring for another patient and would be over around 1:30 PM.

I sat on the edge of his hospital bed massaging his right arm, which was unaffected by his three strokes starting in 1994. He was not awake, but I knew he felt me there. I talked to him anyway. I noticed he gurgled when he breathed in, and I knew what that meant, without anyone telling me. I pushed it out of my mind and kept thinking, "He'll wake up during his bath and everything will be fine." It was a Friday and after the Aid gave him his bath, I knew she would change the sheets. This being the case I figured we'd be good for the weekend. I had made him a "power shake." It was still in the refrigerator untouched but I planned on trying to get him to drink it as soon as I returned from my errands, hopefully he would be feeling a bit better after his bath and clean sheets. I was ready for us to spend a nice weekend together.

My aunt from out of state called and asked to come out for the weekend. My first response was "Not a good idea" since I knew she'd want us all to go out to eat or shop. She just didn't understand what was happening. I told her to come out but not to expect any entertainment outside the house. She said she'd arrive around 1:00 PM or 2:00 PM.

The Aid arrived around 1:45 PM and I left to do my errands, figuring I had about 45 minutes. I did this very quickly, driving too fast but being careful. I just wanted to get home to Hazen. I arrived home and parked the car in the garage. Since the garage was right beneath the living room, I knew he and our two shelties would hear the garage door open and close. I knew this was not going to happen today. I drug my minimal purchases through the work room, dodging tools, benches etc. and up the 14 steps to the kitchen where Hazen and our two shelties always greeted me. I dumped the small bag on the counter and went to see how his sponge bath was going. I watched as the Aid was finishing. I immediately noticed that his bottom was fiery red. I asked the Aid if it was a rash. She said " I wish you had not seen that." Needless to say, his body was beginning to shut down.

After two days of Hazen's eyes being constantly closed, his eyes suddenly flew open. I could tell at this point due to the film on his eyes that he was blind. I ignored it, thinking he'd be fine. He was doing "air kisses." Stupid me! I thought he was thirsty. We had little sponges on sticks that you dipped in water to somewhat quench his thirst. I put one in his mouth, then another. He kept doing "air kisses." I sat down beside him and gave him a kiss. He kissed me back. His head turned to the side and a small amount of brown liquid came out of his mouth. He was GONE! Still not wanting to believe this, I sat there, holding him and "willing him to wake up." "Hell, we had been through 3 strokes, a heart attack, and a quadruple bypass. We can fix this. I sat watching him and kept willing him to wake up.

The aid put her hand on his heart, took his blood pressure and then took me aside and told me he was gone. I ran to his bedside and screamed "NO!!! I held him, wrapped my arms around him and cried like I had never done before. What I felt, no words can possibly describe. I felt as if someone had torn my very soul from my body. I cried that day more than I did when my parents unexpectedly split up, more than when my dad passed away. I didn't scream or yell, the shock was just too much. After all he had been through, I thought he'd "snap out of it" as he had always done before. That he would get better like he always did. The county coroner arrived to pronounce him dead. I hugged him again and finally realized he was cold. I didn't care. He went cold quickly but I just clung to him. The funeral attendants then came to place him in a body bag. I was in the kitchen filling out the paperwork when I suddenly realized what they were doing. I asked them to unwrap the bag for me so I could kiss him one more time. He was cold and waxy at this point but I still didn't care. I just wanted to kiss him one more time. Some people would have shuddered at the feeling, but this was the person I loved for 33 years. We both had faults, but we deeply loved each other no matter what.

Looking back, my life "began" when I met Hazen. It was a very short 33 years. We met inside an amusement park. He and his partner, J.B., made hand carved wax candles. I worked as a photographer taking "old time"pictures"at a concession owned by a photographer. We would dress people in vintage costumes, develop the film and then show them the finished picture with a mat and frame. The whole "pitch" was to sell you either a mat or frame. That's where the money was. We would have contests to see who would sell the most mats and frames. I always worked until closing because I knew Hazen was there, plus I usually had the best sales, getting the tired families at the end of the night to spend more money. These photos were definitely a keepsake for the families that purchased them.

Our booths were almost side by side. (Hazen's booth and my booth). A glass blowers booth was in between us. In the beginning, I just lived to see Hazen walk by and everyone I worked with knew I had a crush on him. The park opened on weekends in April and went full time in June. By then, most of us "craft people" were friendly with each other and we'd stop by each other's booths to talk. I only worked 40 hours a week, but Hazen and J.B. didn't have employees so they worked 12 to 13 hours a day, seven days a week. They also lived in a van on the campground nearby. Sometime in July, J.B.'s family came to visit so he took a few days off which left Hazen alone.

Needing money, I asked if he'd like me to come in a few hours on my time off to help him, thus giving him a much needed break. It worked out well and we worked together like it was the most natural thing in the world.

Since he hadn't even had a partial day off in quite awhile, a few weeks later, I told him that I was getting off early and he should tell JB he was going to take the evening off since I was going to "kidnap" him for an evening. He laughed, but I was serious, so I just kid napped him. We ended up going to a huge rose garden with a thermos of wine and some pizza, and sat across from the park on a hill watching the park close up, being glad for some time off.

That fall, Hazen went home for two weeks to get his affairs in order, promising to be back. Needless to say, it was a teary "so long for now" moment.

I took a job at a convention center, as a bartender and banquet server which I couldn't stand.

After a very long two weeks, Hazen finally returned. He moved all the candle equipment into my basement which was part of a rented house where I lived at the time. After work and on my days off all winter long, he taught me how to make hand carved candles. He was always looking for something wherever we went to pour wax into as a mold. He came up with three new designs that winter. He had also contacted gift shops before he had left and sold wholesale to them. Between the two of us, we could eat and pay the bills.

We went back to the amusement park the following spring. We had gone in early to set up our area that Hazen had designed. During the winter a store had gone out of business and we bought one of their display cases which would normally hold jewelry, so it had shelves inside.

We filled the display case with flood lights and at night we were lit up like a Christmas tree, plus we had a great spot. You couldn't miss us! We paid rent to the park based on the attendance, but they paid the electric and air conditioning that year so we made pretty good money in the end even though it was a lot of hard work. The next year, Hazen put up a plywood wall behind our carving stands. We brought in a sleeping bag, a small refrigerator and wind chimes so we could take breaks without really leaving each other alone. Hazen always worked the opening of the park shift, while I rested. By the third summer I noticed that he would just sit and talk to people but not make any candles. A few months before, I had taken him for a check up and the doctor said he had high blood pressure and put him on medication. Hazen was very outgoing and loved to be around people. When I would finish resting and it was his turn to rest, I was overwhelmed with custom made candle orders, re stocking the candles which were sold, and everything had to be finished before the next rush around 5 or 6 PM.

It was a perfect working relationship. Hazen would take care of the customers and I would quietly sit on the other side at my carving stand making candles. We finally had to hire high school kids to come in and just dip the candles in the hot wax so I could keep up.

We were at the park for 8 years, eight wonderful fun years. We met a lot of people, made friends that we kept in touch with and all of a sudden the "powers that be" in charge of merchandise realized we were making a lot of money in the spot we had and they wanted it badly. So they moved us to another location and we lost our income.

Hazen had done contract painting years before and said he would teach me. Through a friend who did window treatments, we found out about a new upper middle class housing community that needed painters. We painted one house and were hired on the spot. Between all of us, from the Realtor to the Carpenter, plumbers, carpet layers, and landscapers, we had a House finished in a month and a half. It was breakneck speed and many times we had to speed up even more just to keep up. We'd go a few days not sleeping or eating, chain smoking, grinding our teeth, just to get the house finished. Then it all came to a screeching halt. The owner of the community went bankrupt. He had been given the land by his grandfather but blew the money, owing everyone thousands of dollars, us included.

By then, we lived a few towns away in a townhouse for much higher rent than our previous small apartment. My aunt sent us rent money for a month. Hazen kept asking the maintenance Supervisor to hire us to paint the apartments and townhouses. Hazen once told me he got a job just because he badgered the guy so much. Sure enough it worked and we were the painters for a 688 unit apartment/townhouse community.

Hazen was always in a rock and roll band. Somehow he kept finding people and making a new band. When someone would drop out, they would be replaced with another person. It was continuous. This went on from the time we had started doing candles through the painting jobs. I did get irritated a few times since Hazen always had to do the leg work and most of our money went into the bands. Although when I saw him on stage singing, playing the guitar or keyboard, my heart melted. That was what he was meant to do. He and the band performed for the MDA Telethon for a few years with all donations going to help fight muscular dystrophy. He was a total showman, either on the stage or "smoozing" the customers in the park selling our candles.

My dad had remarried and decided he liked his new wife's home better than his, so he told us he would give us his house (along with my brother who lived about 15 hours away) but we had to go there at least once a month and tend to things, like weeding, mowing and in general make it look nice.

We went to dad's house once a month. Hazen and his band played at local places at least twice a month which left us with one weekend free. We were always on the go. One weekend we were packing up to go to my dad's for Thanksgiving and Hazen asked me if he looked funny. He always had a crooked smile, so I didn't think too much about it. Then he said he had no feeling in his left arm. My neighbor rushed us to the hospital. Hazen's blood pressure was 250/150. Not knowing anything about strokes, I had no clue what was happening except that Hazen was not feeling well and I didn't know how to help him. He had suffered a stroke. He spent a long week in the hospital. The day he came home he was to call his doctor to set up an MRI. As he was talking to the doctor, the doctor asked him how he was feeling. He said "I feel fine but my left arm is numb.

The doctor sent him back to the hospital. His blood pressure was back up to 250/150. The staff thought the machine was broken so they checked it again manually. The machine was not broken, he had suffered another stroke. Why? Why was this happening? Was it our lifestyle? On the go all the time? Fast food?

His first two strokes were considered "reversible," through physical therapy, and a change of medicine. He came home two weeks later. Hazen always hired band members to help us paint, so the latest guy and I kept painting, leaving Hazen home alone. Fortunately, we lived in the same community where we painted, so I was able to go home and check on him throughout the day. After a few months Hazen was able to come back to work. He worked slowly at first and eventually full time hours. The band guy was offered a good paying job and quit, so Hazen and I continued to paint on our own. Everything seemed fine. We worked together, went away one weekend to dad's house, and puttered in the cool mountain air. We had dinner out in the Golf Resort dad managed. Life was calm. We even celebrated two years stroke free.

That New Years Eve we worked until noon, bought Hazen a new computer chair and did enough grocery shopping to last us a few days. We came home. Hazen put his new computer chair together and then said he had a bad headache. I thought maybe it was from not eating so I made a salad and some steamed shrimp. After he ate, I had him take a hot shower, thinking maybe it was a sinus headache. He finished his shower. I laid pillows on the floor in front of the TV and made sure he was comfortable and went to take my shower. When I left him he was laying on his back, with his feet toward the TV. When I returned after my shower, he was on his stomach, left hand curled on his lower back and lying in a different direction. I woke him and he said he needed the bathroom. His left side just would not cooperate. I held him up in the bathroom, but he kept insisting I let him alone. When I let go, he just slumped to the floor. After going to the bathroom, I got him back to the living room and gave him two choices. I either call an ambulance or call our friend Kelly to take him back to the hospital. He had a fit about going back to the hospital since we still owed them money from his two previous strokes.

Their billing department would call and actually scream

over the phone that we were late on a payment. I ended up calling Kelly. (Kelly and her husband were our friends, not close, but for some reason I called her anyway. She ended up being one of the best friends I ever had in my life.) When Kelly arrived, she took one look at him and said "Call the ambulance." Again, Hazen had a fit. She told him if he didn't cooperate, she'd pick him up and carry him to her car and take him. Hazen later told me he thought Kelly was really strong enough to pick him up and carry him to the car. The ambulance arrived in a few minutes, loaded him up and off they went. Kelly and I following behind.

This time, his blood pressure was 165/155 and again, they thought the machine was broken. He was in the hospital for two months, going back and forth from the hospital to the rehab area.

I would work from 7:30 AM to 2 PM, go home, shower and be at the hospital by 3:15 PM every day.

One afternoon I happened to arrive at the hospital earlier than usual. As I approached his room, I noticed 5 nurses in the hallway just outside his room talking about their weddings. I walked into his room to see him tied spread eagle on the bed, stark naked and the bed full of urine. The nurse's call button connected to the bed was shut OFF and the other call button attached to a cord was put on a table naturally out of his reach. After I asked the 5 nurses who was in charge of Hazen, another nurse came in.

She actually said these words to me: "Oh Mrs. Meek, you weren't supposed to see him like this. Do you want to clean him up? I have all the clean sheets and gown." I was too busy seeing red, not to mention absolutely furious and not wanting to upset Hazen, you guessed it, yeah, I cleaned everything up. He had called me the night before telling me the nurse was mad and threatened to turn off the call button because he wanted some water. I truly thought it was the medicine talking at the time. For what kind of nurse would do that to someone? Isn't a nurse a human being? Doesn't someone go into nursing knowing they take care of people? It has been proven to me over and over again that some of these people are in the wrong profession.

While he was in the hospital but allowed to be in the wheel chair, he'd roam around the ICU floor. There was a sensor on his chair and if he left that area an alarm would go off. He figured out where the alarms were and watched a nurse put in the code. Well, that's all it took, he'd wheel past the alarm, put in the code and off he went. He didn't leave the floor, but you just weren't sure where he was at times. At night before I left I would take him downstairs where the cafeteria was to get him a chocolate frozen yogurt. One night as we were heading to a table a nurse was sitting at a table with her back to us. Since she still had scrubs and booties on we figured she had just finished up in the ER. Just as we were passing her, she left out a tremendous fart. Hazen turned to me saying in a loud voice, "Did you hear that?" We were both laughing so hard at our table and he kept repeating it so we'd laugh all the harder. The poor woman, just sat there making no attempt to leave. It's not like we would ever see her again or even recognize her. After the third stroke, he needed a shunt put in his head to release the pressure. He was completely out of it for two to three days. I kept wanting to talk to the neurosurgeon to find out what was happening. The nurses were also getting agitated that he wouldn't wake up or talk to me. When he finally woke up, the nurses had just had enough and paged the neurosurgeon. He came in the room, huffing and puffing, walks up to me and says "WHAT?" I had told Hazen that Dr. Dick was going to come by to talk to us. Hazen was in a room with 5 other beds near the nurse's station so the patients could all be monitored. Dr. Dick (of course not his real name but it did start with a D and I came to realize later that it was his nick name.) He talked jibberish to us and walked away. As he was leaving, the room, Hazen asked me loudly if that was Dr. Dick? The nurses cracked up and that's when I knew for sure it was a nickname and it really suited him.

After two and a half months, Hazen came home in a wheelchair. Since our townhouse had a curb and a long sidewalk with steps, Kelly and I had to learn from Rehab how to maneuver the wheelchair up the steps to get it into the townhouse.

Hazen was due home! Nothing had been set up to take care of him after he did come home, so I paid Kelly to care for him in the mornings while I painted the majority of the apartments. When I came home, I would take care of Hazen and Kelly would finish the trim in the apartments for me.

I kept calling Social Services/Assisted Living Agencies to get help. Assisted Living assured me they would have someone come out all three times I called, but nobody came. I finally got through to another Assisted Living Agency and they sent a man over who was epileptic and he would have seizures. That was certainly not helpful, plus the guy shouldn't have been driving. The organization even left the man drive patients to and from doctor appointments.

He did drive Hazen to one appointment and had a seizure on the way home. He took his foot off the gas and fortunately Hazen steered the car off the road. We were on a two lane road with a school bus behind us. Frantically, I waved to the bus driver to slow down. The man came out of his seizure and we continued home. It was getting close to Christmas and painting was slow and I knew we would be home for at least the next week, so I cancelled the services with the Assisted Living Agency for that week. Finally, I told the agency I preferred someone else. A middle aged woman came to the house and she was great. She took good care of Hazen, did laundry, and kept him entertained for two hours a day while I worked.

Hazen had wonderful OT and PT nurses who came to the townhouse to work with him. Between them and the Assisted Living attendants, for once I was comfortable going to work. We were so far in debt I really had to work. Between PT plus what he had accomplished on his own before they came to our aid, he was able to climb the steps to our bedroom. (Which was one of his goals.) He also was able to climb in and out of the bathtub. Life got a little easier for both of us. When Hazen was in the hospital I had decided to make a quilt out of our old clothes. I'd cut up the squares at home at night after visiting him at the hospital. When I was at the hospital I would sew the squares together, come home and sew the squares onto a bigger piece, then cut more squares. Our friends gave us a daybed since he was still in a wheel chair and confined to the first floor of the townhouse once he came home. At night I would pull the daybed next to the couch so we could at least sleep side by side. At this point all I had to do was sew the top piece with all the squares, the matting and the sheet I used as the underside.

As I was sitting on the couch hand sewing the quilt. I'd toss part of it over him while he slept.

One night, he was sleeping with his back to me and I'm sewing like mad to get it finished. He rolled over and the whole quilt went with him. I had unknowingly sewed his pajama top into the bottom of the quilt. He always enjoyed telling people how I sewed him into the quilt and was glad I had "unsewed" him so he wasn't hanging on the quilt rack. While it is very serious having strokes and spending part of your life in a hospital, we still tried our hardest to have a little fun.

We stayed where we were in the townhouse for a few years while still painting for the apartment community. A new Maintenance Supervisor was hired and we just plain didn't hit it off. One day we had a blow up and I quit. Stupid. But I did. I sold all our paint equipment to the new painter. He brought in a crew to help him paint the following week to paint a three bedroom townhouse. What we did in an hour and a half, it took them a day and a half to do.

I then took a job in a retail store, then a grocery store, and eventually went back to bar tending, since we didn't work at the apartment community anymore and we now had to pay "real rent." For the thirteen years we had worked there, they froze our rent. It wasn't because we were fabulous painters. It was because we were reliable and cheap.

On my way to work each morning, I kept passing this very "funky" house. One day as I was passing it, it had a FOR SALE sign in the front yard. It looked like a house with a half house butted next to it. It looked like it had two front doors, Strange but cute. We knew a realtor and called him to set up an appointment to look at the house that Friday afternoon.

While we were driving over, I told him not to get excited and not to show a deep interest in the house even if he loved it. We toured the house on our own. It had an eat in kitchen with a window, a full bathroom with a window. We never had that at the townhouse. There was a large living room with a fireplace, windows on each end of the room. All rooms except the bathroom had ceiling fans. It had a heated garage, workroom, finished off basement, large dining room, two bedrooms and a huge attic. All I wanted was for Hazen to live on one floor, no steps to go to bed or a bath. When we were finished the Realtor asked what we thought. "We'll take it." I blurted out. Hazen just looked at me and reminded me of what I had said to him about not being so excited. We put money down and signed the papers that very same day.

A month later we started moving in. I would drop things off at our new home on the way to work each day. I remember the first thing I dropped off was our fake Christmas tree. We were both so excited! Our first Christmas in our new home and a fireplace! Because we really couldn't believe this was happening to us, we really didn't check out the house in detail. We hadn't noticed the long piece of duct tape in the kitchen nor were we aware of the measurements of the rooms. We didn't care. It was our first home with a yard for our cocker spaniel (a rescue dog) named Kody. Because our headboard on the bed was too big for the bedrooms, we ended up sleeping in the attic. Having to go to the bathroom in the middle of the night, being all google eyed was not safe for either of us. That spring I had the dining room partitioned off with a wall and door to make it our bedroom. All we had to do to go to the bathroom was make a left, take three steps and there we were. Yes… things were going good again. Although Hazen was home alone, at least there were no steps to worry about now.

He spent one day polishing all the brass doorknobs, another organizing cabinets, another setting up the computer room. He loved to putter in this house. In the summer I would dress him in a light colored T shirt and shorts. One day after I came home from work and after our kissing, I followed him around the house. I noticed the back of his T shirt was dirty. We walked outside from the back porch and I noticed a ladder leaning against the roof over the porch and a broom on the porch roof "Hmmm, Hazen, did you fall off the roof?" I asked. He said, "No, I was cleaning the gutters." I replied, "so, when did you fall?" He said "While I was cleaning the gutters." Well, I realized I couldn't allow this to happen, so the next day we went to the hardware store and got a gutter cleaner that hooks up to a garden hose allowing you to clean the gutters while staying on the ground. Even though he was unable to work, he was a "doer" and hated being idle. He thought that since I worked, that meant he had to also.

He loved vacuuming, so I got him a pet specialized vacuum. He cut the grass so it looked like a golf course. He did laundry, washed dishes, polished and dusted everything. All I did was bar tend from 10:30 AM . Sometimes until midnight if the motel forgot to hire another bar tender for a special event.

One morning about 4 AM he got up to use the bathroom. I always woke up when he got out of bed. He was coming back to the bedroom and passed out face down onto the hardwood floor. He sounded like a wounded animal. He howled kind of quietly, then louder. I flew out of bed and saw blood all over the floor. I grabbed a bunch of towels and called 911. Fortunately his head did not hit the piano which was just inches away.

Again, I didn't know what to do, so I sat him up, using as many towels as I could find waiting for the ambulance. Since he swallowed so much blood and I had sat him up, he began throwing up blood. I followed the ambulance in our car, through a freak snow storm, sliding all over the road and thanking God there were no other drivers out. The ER staff got him into a bed, started checking his vitals when a nurse came in for a minute and then quickly left. Hazen threw up again. I looked for anything to clean him up and then got reprimanded for doing anything. I was told I should have waited for someone…. ? When another nurse came in all she did was complain about how bad Hazen's breath was. Well of course his breath was bad, he had been throwing up blood! When he fell, he broke his nose in three places and since this hospital had no Ear, Nose Throat Specialist, they shipped him off to another hospital. His nose got packed,

Xrays were taken and he was to be released in two days. As it turned out, one of his blood pressure meds stopped working and that is what caused him to pass out.

Before he was released, I had gone to the hospital pharmacy to pick up his new medications. At that time, the nurse took out the nose packing and he bled out badly. He ended up having a micro mini pad complete with a string in his nose. They taped the string to his cheek. You'd think that in a hospital where people have many different ailments that have caused them to be there, nobody would stare at another patient.

Well, people do stare. People were staring horribly at my poor Hazen with his Racoon face and a string taped to his cheek as he was being wheeled out of the hospital. I stared each one of them down until they looked away in shame.

Thank goodness his teeth survived. The dentist said no teeth were broken at that point, but most of his top teeth were bad and soon would need to be pulled. After his broken nose had healed up and he lost his racoon face, we were off to the dentist to get the bad teeth removed. (Right before Hazen's mother passed away, she had complained about his teeth. I promised her I would take care of that.) And I did. He would need a partial plate but that could not be fitted for two weeks, so while his gums healed, we both ate soft foods. His face healed and he got a new partial plate. He looked great!

A few months later as I was getting ready for work on a Sunday morning, Hazen said he wasn't feeling well at all, so I decided to call off (I never do that.) As I was on the phone he came up behind me and passed out, pulling me, the phone and the table to the floor with him. I called and made an appointment with a cardiologist. This was in the fall and it was cool, so I had put a sweatshirt on him to go to the doctors.

When we got in to see the doctor, Hazen started sweating badly. I pulled off the sweatshirt, but he was stiff as a board, saying he wanted to sit down. We couldn't make him sit because he was so rigid. The doctor turned to me and said, "I think he is having a heart attack." He then calls out to the receptionist to call 911. Even though the doctors office is right behind the hospital, it took the ambulance twenty minutes to get there. Sure enough, he had a heart attack with ninety percent blockage, which meant open heart surgery and later a pacemaker. I knew he would be drugged up, but went to the hospital anyway for a good luck kiss. All he had been through and he never gave up. Not once!

Written by Hazen Meek

CHAPTER 1

I stand about 5 feet 10 inches tall and weigh approximately 135 lbs. I am 67 years old. I have steel gray hair and its been said that I look like Albert Einstein's brother. I am the baby of five children (one sister and three brothers.) I was a typical child with no outstanding traits or talents. Truthfully, there really is nothing outstanding about me other than being a "curiosity" to others. I worshiped my mother and father. They were my whole world.

My father was a prominent attorney in a medium size southern town. Although he worked very hard, he always found time for family. As a child, I used to go to his office on a regular basis with my mother. I would marvel at his big desk and remember thinking he had to be a very important man to have a secretary to help him with his work load. My father also had a fetish for silver dollars. He always had at least a dozen or so in his pocket and would rarely part with one unless someone in the family did something extra special.

One afternoon while visiting my father's office, I scooted past his secretary and slipped into his office and hopped up on his big leather chair. I propped my feet up on his desk. I leaned back in the chair and nonchalantly looked up at the ceiling. My eyes suddenly became fixed on something on the ceiling. At this time, my father entered the room and acknowledged me.

Being the curious child that I was, I asked him "What is that?" My father answered, "Well son, that is a twenty dollar bill." I was baffled as to why a twenty dollar bill would be taped to the ceiling. Then he continued on, "Son, I am an attorney who deals with broken marriages. Some can be fixed and some cannot. The people who come to me with that problem come in with their heads bowed as if ashamed, so I took a twenty dollar bill and wrapped it around a silver dollar. I then placed a piece of tape around it in such a manner that when I tossed it up to the ceiling the silver dollar would return to me and the twenty dollar bill would stay stuck to the ceiling." (Please note that in 1953 there was no such thing as double sided tape.) He then said, "If anyone other than family comes into my office and notices it, I will take it down and give it to them."

A few months later, while visiting his office I noticed the twenty dollar bill was gone from the ceiling. My father told me that the only person who noticed it was the cleaning lady, so he climbed up on his desk, took it down and gave it to her. I will leave it to you to figure out the moral of my father's story. It took me many years to figure it out, but eventually I did.

In 1953, at age 9, little did I know that my world was

about to be suddenly turned upside down. It was the first real change in my life.

Though it is still painful even at age 67 to be writing about my father, his story must be told. It is important to tell his story because it has a large impact on my story and this will become apparent as you read.

My dad became ill and had to sleep in the downstairs bedroom and only when he came out of his bedroom could we spend time together, so each minute was precious. I will never forget this one particular day. It is burned into my memory never to be erased. My dad and I were joking, laughing and having a great time. He even spun me around in his chair. I knew what came next was to listen to the Fireside Theater or The Shadow on the radio and then some music. Dad suddenly got up and said he had to call his secretary on urgent business.

I looked on as he went into the den to call his office, knowing he would be back in just a few minutes. In the midst of my mother telling me that he was talking to his secretary, all of a sudden I heard him cry out "Louise" (my mother's name). She then ran into the den. (At a later time in my life, she told me that he had handed her the phone and fell back into her arms.) I heard my mother yelling for the boys which was normal in our household. I waited and waited for dad, but when he did not come out of the den nor did I hear his booming voice, I walked over to the den and opened the door. There he was, laying on the floor with medics standing all around him. Seeing them shaking their heads and my mother in tears told it all. I ran into the dining room and prayed, and prayed, AND PRAYED but to no avail. It was apparently God's decision that dad was finished with his job on earth. This certainly was no comfort to a nine year old child who had just lost everything. Being so young, I was totally devastated and confused.

What had happened was dad had suffered a heart attack. His heart just burst in his chest. Since my dad had heart problems we all had been told what was coming but that did not lessen the pain of losing him. It wasn't until years later that I realized where my writing skills came from. I know in my heart they came from heaven above.

After my dad died, I had a great deal of trouble sleeping, so I would get up in the early morning hours and go to the kitchen, get a glass of milk and scribble my thoughts on a pad of paper.

At age 9 with tears running down my cheeks onto the paper and my heart splitting into what felt like a million pieces, this is what I wrote:

IS IT RIGHT?

Is it right to go through life with a hope and goal in mind?
To step off in an endless sleep and leave all your work behind?

Is it right to go on loving each and every day?
And then to leave your love behind when you surely pass away?

Is it right to believe in something that you have never seen?

With each hour and day passing as if it was a dream?

Yes, it is right to go through life with a hope and
goal in mind.
So youth can take up after you and strive to make
their lives sublime.

Yes, it is right to go on loving each and every day
and then to leave your love behind.

For you leave your love and memories which can
never die with time.

My mother found it the next morning and asked me if I
wrote it, which I did. She then surprised me by asking me if
I would try to write one for her. I told her that I really didn't
know where the words came from, that they just came out,
but that I would try! What a mystery. After all, what is it
that causes a small child to become inspired? It seemed to
me that after losing my dad, this was a way to ease the pain
and pressure, so for the next three or four weeks, I tried to
write a poem for my mother. I had almost given up hope
when one morning I awoke and wrote the poem called "One
Child" for my mother.

ONE CHILD

A child wished upon a star one night and thought
of things to be.
He thought of how the world was and how it was
meant to be.

He thought of how the world would be if
God were here today.
And then he knelt upon his knees and silently he
did pray.

He prayed for us in every way in hopes that we
might live.
In hopes that we would go on each day and give to
God what we were meant to give,

For this child who prayed for you and me, should
cause us to think twice.
For this child was sent from God above. His name
was Jesus Christ.

Now, I am not a professional author but because I was so lonely after my dad's passing, I started writing and continued writing up until my last stroke.

Shortly after my dad passed, my mother enrolled me in Military School. Years later I served in the U.S. Navy and married. The marriage failed. At the age of 53, after my first stroke, I went back to college and graduated as a Computer Servicing Technologist. All were life changing experiences, some good, some bad. Little did I know that later in my life I would experience yet another life changing experience. One that would change my life forever, (as you will see as you read on.)

CHAPTER 2

After serving my tour in the U.S. Navy and returning home to Tennessee, a friend called me and asked if I would like to be a partner in a business venture selling Hand Carved Candles. He told me he had a contract for a retail stand located in the Craft Barn inside of Hershey Park in Hershey, PA. The Amusement Park had originally been built by the founder of Hershey Foods, Milton S. Hershey and was intended to be used only for Hershey Park workers and their families, but was now open to the public. I told him I was definitely interested but had no idea how to make a hand carved candle. He assured me that he could teach me. He asked me to pack up and move to his home in Hershey and help him get things ready, so I did. Upon arrival, we needed to build a stand plus a display case. He had the measurements needed and the equipment so I set up the lay out and design and went to work. This was quite a challenging task since the stand had to have a professional look rather than your typical flea market look to uphold the standards of the park.

So to create a stand and display case seemed almost like an oxymoron, not to mention the fact that a lighting system would also be needed to display the candles properly. None the less, I was up to the challenge.

I designed it in a horse shoe shape with carving stands that allowed three to five people deep to observe the actual carving of the candles. The days were long and hard since my partner was also showing me how to carve candles at that time. I even designed a candle on my own. I called it the Love Light Candle. It was beautiful. It had hearts all around it with a star on top. The light shone throughout the center of the candle's carved hearts enhancing its color.

I also added sayings such as: I Love you with the name of the person the candle was intended for.

After we finished construction of the display case and the stand, we packed up and moved everything to Hershey Park and set it up. We had everything ready to go a few days before opening day of the park. We tried to keep our prices reasonable so everyone could afford a candle for a loved one or themselves. After a few months we discovered our "new business" venture was quite profitable. Little did I realize then that I would once again go through another life changing event in the very near future.

There was another stand not far from ours. The woman who ran this stand was a photographer and made Sepia Tone color pictures. She would have her customers dress in various vintage costumes and photograph them and then sell them their pictures. One evening she was browsing our candle stand and asked if we could use a gal at our stand to handle customers. It seemed her stand was not doing well and she could no longer retain all of her helpers. I told her to send them down and we would try it to see if it would work out. A beautiful young lady named Linda was the first to stop by. We both felt she would be good, so we hired her. I took her phone number and wrote it in the notebook I always kept with me so we could call her to come to work when we needed her.

One evening when we were particularly busy, my partner told me he was not coming back at the end of the season because of the long hours we had to put in making candles. I could relate! Sometimes we would put in 15 to 18 hours a day at the Candle stand plus an additional 3 to 4 hours a day making candles for the next day. Though our business was thriving, the hours were grueling to say the least. He asked me if I wanted to take on the contract myself and I said "yes." He explained that the long hours took him away from his family too much and he needed to move on. At the end of the season, I decided to move back to Tennessee for awhile. I wasn't really sure if I could handle the contract on my own but I was certainly going to try. Then it hit me! I realized that I still had Linda's phone number, so a day before arriving in Hershey, PA I called her. I asked her if she could find a place for me to store my equipment and also try to find a place for me to stay, because I had several candle orders to fill and deliver.

She told me to call her once I got to Hershey, so I did. Upon reaching Hershey, she asked me to come over to her house and she took me to a side door which led to the basement. It was empty except for a couch. She said the couch opened into a bed and that I could sleep there temporarily until I found a place to rent. She also said I could store my equipment there. Since Linda worked during the day I could make the candles and fill some of the gift shop orders I had taken the year before I left for Tennessee. These orders needed to be delivered before the park opened for the season.

Linda was a true lady and set up the rules. Since I absolutely had no romantic wants or desires due to the failure of my first marriage, (although I did find her sweet and beautiful) I readily agreed. Also the contract came first. She was very considerate and left the door to the upstairs open while she was at work in case I needed to use the rest room or bathe.

One evening after she came home from work, she knocked on the basement door. I was in the process of making some candles and carving them. She asked me if I could teach her. She seemed so fascinated with the whole process, so of course I said "yes." The following evening I started her out with blank wax, dipping the candle with the colors she chose. I started with the simplest ones first and had her observe me as I carved them. I explained that she would be ready to start carving the next day. The next day I had her dip the same number of coats of wax, but with no color (figuring that if she messed it up, it would be no loss). I was concerned that she might get discouraged should things not go well. I was amazed that she picked up so quickly. I later learned that she had attended an art college and that was the reason for this. Over the next few weeks, we moved on to more difficult designs. Once again she did well. Slowly but surely she learned how the temperature of the wax could work in her favor. As I began watching her intently I suddenly realized how nice it was just to have someone to talk to and trust.

Finally it was getting close to the time for Hershey Park to open. I knew that Linda had mastered the art of candle carving and I knew that we needed to talk. After she arrived home from work one evening I asked her if we could talk and of course her response was "About what?" I asked her if she had a job for that coming summer and she said "no." I then asked " Would you like to work with me?" I told her to think seriously about that question and then ask anything she wished. I told her that if her answer was yes, then I had another question I wanted her to consider. She said "yes" to the first question. Then all of a sudden a look came over her face as if it was the dreaded question most women fear, but I continued on. My words to her were this: "If you work with me, I would consider you a partner." She said " But I cannot afford that." I told her there would be no funds required and that I just needed someone to back me up whom I could trust. I told her that if I brought in $100, as my partner, her share would be 50 percent of the take in, minus expenses owed to the park. YES! Things were finally looking up. I now had a partner who was not afraid of the customers, or hard work and also did beautiful work.

Later that summer, I was notified that the divorce from my former wife had become final. I suddenly realized that I had fallen deeply in love with Linda and knew I wanted her to be my wife. Towards the end of the season, I bought a bottle of wine and some pizza and asked Linda to accompany me up to the hill near the park. She agreed. After we settled into our little "picnic" like area, I knelt down on my knees and proposed to her. Her answer was "NO." I was stunned but thought maybe it was because she didn't know me well enough yet. Apparently the question came as such a shock that she threw up some of the pizza. I thought to myself, "maybe pizza and wine were not a good choice of mixes." I told her my offer would remain open unless one of us decided to end the relationship. I found out later that Linda really did love me, she just didn't want to be the "rebound chick" as she called it. The last month for the park was upon us and I was right in the middle of making a 12 inch candle when Linda interrupts and says "Do you remember that question you asked me when we were up on the hill?" I said "yes." She then says, "My answer is yes!" I was bubbling over with such excitement that my hands began to tremble and Yep! You guessed it I destroyed that candle. "Oh well", I thought, "there will be other candles but there will only ever be one Linda."

Being the proper young man I was, I then called her father and asked him to meet us for lunch. Over lunch, I told him that I had fallen in love with his daughter and wanted his permission to marry her. (I figured it was best to cover all the channels at the time.) We were married in a Methodist Church in Hershey three years later. For our special day I made a Unity Candle with the following words on it "When Two Hearts Touch Love Begins." "When Two Hearts Intertwine Love is Forever." As of this writing, we have been married 30 years.

Shortly after we married, I awoke one morning to see two men walking around the neighbor's yard. It seemed very suspicious to me, so I got dressed and went outside.

I asked one of them if I could help him and he said he was just looking for the candle maker who had candles in the Hershey Gift Shop. (Linda and I often received requests from the Gift Shop for our candles and of course we provided them.) I said "oh, you must mean my wife and I." After a brief conversation, he said he had someone out in the car who would like to meet me and asked me to walk to the car with him. Upon reaching the car, the door flew open and a woman's hand suddenly grabbed my hand. She said, "I am so very sorry to bother you on your day off but I am only going to be here a short time and I would like to purchase some of your candles." She introduced herself as the daughter of the President of the United States. (I'm not sure if it's permissible to mention her name or the president's name so I refrain from doing so in this writing.) But I assure you she was the president's daughter! I escorted her into our home and seated her in the living room. I asked if she would mind waiting a few moments and she said "no, that would be fine." I stood at the bottom of the stairs and called out to Linda and told her we had company. Her reply was "Who have you brought home now?" I told her I had the daughter of the President of the United States of America downstairs and that she wanted to purchase some candles. A blood curdling scream echoed though out the house. Within just a few minutes, Linda appeared all dressed up, hair fixed and make up on. She looked like a model that had just stepped out of a magazine. I was truly amazed at how little time it took her to get herself together because it usually took at least 25 minutes for her to get ready for me. I guess it is just one of those "woman things."

CHAPTER 3

Eventually we were forced to quit the candle business since the wax we used was a petroleum product. The cost of gas went up as well as the cost of the wax.

After quitting the candle business, my wife and I started a painting business, painting apartments and homes. Both the candle business and the painting business were successful, the painting business being the greater of the two. As a painting contractor, we worked for a home builder, painting his newly built homes and later three large apartment communities. Life was good but extremely busy for both of us that year. Not only did I work as a painting contractor during the day, I also was the lead vocalist in a Rock and Roll Band at night. The new band needed a name. They seemed to think my name was so unique that it was impossible for any other band to have that name. They also felt we were unique and wanted our name to be unique too. I nearly died laughing when the group (by unanimous decision) decided to call us "Hazen."

We played in many of the night clubs in the area and also did a number of Muscular Dystrophy telethons to help raise money for Muscular Dystrophy. Between painting all day, practicing or playing for the clubs at night, there wasn't much time for fun. I was a heavy smoker typical junk food eater and running on adrenalin most of the time. At the time I didn't realize, these three things would have such an adverse effect on my life in the future. I was young and thought I had the world by the butt. I felt invincible! I felt as if I could do anything. I was on a roll and life was good!

It was 1994. We had been booked to play at one of the local bars. It was a Saturday night and we had taken a short break to meet with the audience. After the break, we returned to the stage to start our second set. During the second song, I suddenly became disoriented and dizzy so I sat down. The band members stopped and gathered around me. I told them to continue and that I would be ready to continue in a few minutes. I thought that I had just become over heated due to the heat from the lights and all the singing. After a short period of time I stood up and we continued. We finished the night and went home. I still felt a "little off" so to speak so after we arrived home, I took two aspirins and went straight to bed. The next morning I awoke with a slight headache. Because I had never had a sickness like this before, I disregarded it as some kind of virus. Later on that morning I started to feel like my old self again and gave it no further thought. I should have gone to the doctor, but because I rarely felt that way, life went on. The next few weeks I felt great. I was a little tired but nothing beyond the norm.

The following week was Thanksgiving week and my wife and I were scheduled to go to her father's home for Thanksgiving dinner. After bathing and getting ready for the trip, I noticed my mouth was droopy and all of a sudden I just didn't feel right. Linda called the doctor and he instructed her to take me to the hospital. I was in the hospital for two weeks and then came home. The doctors suspected I had suffered a stroke but more tests were necessary to be sure.

After arriving home, the doctor called to let us know about the test he had scheduled for me the following day. He asked Linda how I was doing. I was laying on the couch at the time when my left hand started to go numb. . Linda informed the doctor of the problem and he told her to take me back to the hospital immediately. After a number of tests the doctor concluded that I had suffered a stroke.

During my second hospital stay, I awoke as a nurse came in with a wheelchair and asked if I wanted a bath. I told her "Yes, that would be nice." She helped me into the wheelchair and rolled me to a large tiled shower room. She then took a hose and sprayed me with a full blast of cold water, then took me back to my room and changed me into dry clothing. On another occasion, she came into the room with a large bag of popcorn, laid the popcorn on the opposite empty bed, sat down and turned on the TV and began watching a soap opera. She didn't say "Hi" or anything for that matter, nor did she offer me any popcorn. She acted as if I wasn't even there. Now my own personal belief is that "nobody should be treated like that, stroke or no stroke." If I knew then what I know now, I would have sued the hospital for her incompetent behavior and unprofessional manner.

After meeting with the doctor the day of my discharge, I knew I had to change my life style immediately. He informed me that I had suffered a stroke. Actually two of them. One on Thanksgiving, and the other after I had returned home from the hospital with the first one. I lost my peripheral vision and only had partial movement of my legs and walking abilities. The doctors attributed it to my blood pressure and the stroke and ordered medication to keep my blood pressure at a normal level. He instructed me to quit smoking, no more junk food and to eat a healthy diet low in cholesterol and low salt. My wife and I immediately changed our eating habits and I quit smoking. I noticed that I had a tendency to drag my left foot. It just didn't seem to want to work the way it was supposed to, so I began exercising daily by walking up and down the sidewalk in front of our home. It was difficult but I figured "Enough of this already!" I wasn't about to give up. I needed to get back to work. We had a painting contract and I felt horrible that my dear wife was trying to paint all those apartments on her own. Within a few months I was able to go back to work. My peripheral vision had returned and I had regained more movement in my legs and feet.

CHAPTER 4

My next stroke happened two years later in 1996. It was New Year's Eve and Linda and I had decided to go shopping for some shrimp to bring in the New Year. We did a lot of shopping and picked up a computer chair since mine was shot. We went home and I put the computer chair together. I had been dealing with a nasty headache all day but thought it was just my sinus's since I do have sinus problems. After getting the computer chair together, I took a shower then nibbled on some shrimp. I then grabbed a blanket and pillow and laid on the floor in front of the TV. After my wife had showered, she came downstairs and found me unconscious, face down, with my fingers curled up and laying in a strange position. My hand and arm were twisted behind my back, almost as if I had suffered a seizure. I was taken to the hospital by a close friend of ours. She and my wife had to help me to the car. Shortly after arrival at the hospital I lost consciousness.

I don't remember being unconscious but I do remember laying face down in the hospital bed trying to pray the Lord's Prayer. I thought the Lord must think me crazy but I just could not remember the words no matter how hard I tried. Though I couldn't remember the words, I knew in my heart that He knew what I was trying to do and would see me through it.

I was placed in ICU and hooked up to almost everything you can imagine. I'm not sure how long I was unconscious but I do know the doctors had to drill a hole in my skull and put a shunt in my brain to relieve the pressure. Once they did, I eventually regained consciousness. You know they say you cannot hear anything when in an unconscious state but THIS IS NOT SO! It was not until later that the nurses told me that when my wife would walk into the room and just touch my hand, my blood pressure would drop into a normal range again. Other times she would just lay on the bed beside me and the nurses noticed this would put me at ease. Somehow I knew her touch and knew I had to fight. Believe it or not, these are the little things that really do help a great deal when one is in an unconscious state. I remember hearing my wife's voice telling me "Hang in there!" "We will whip this thing together." She later told me that she yelled that in my ear while I was unconscious. I thought it was a whisper. But whether it was a yell or a whisper it was the sweetest thing I had ever heard.

This brings back the time when my wife's step father had an accident on the New Jersey Turnpike. He had hit the Medial strip and was laying in a hospital bed. His family came into his room crying and carrying on saying how he was going to die. When my wife and I saw him in his halo cast, I leaned over and whispered in his ear, "Some folks will do anything to get out of work." When he regained consciousness, he had remembered what I had said. In fact, he said we were the only ones he remembered that visited him. So please remember that you must be very careful what you say around someone who is unconscious. Your words can be as dangerous as the wrong medication. When in the presence of an unconscious person, think before you speak, Even though unconscious, that person can still hear everything you say. The mind still functions unless a person is brain dead. I know, because I myself experienced it.

CHAPTER 5

I would now like to share a few things that happened to me while I was in the hospital. Some funny and some not so funny:

After two months in the hospital, I had met a lot of other stroke patients. In fact one was a doctor and his wife. The doctor had suffered a stroke and couldn't remember his name nor the medical field he had been trained in. His poor wife was so lost and despondent and had no idea how to help him. I talked with her about my previous strokes and how I had recovered from them.. I discussed with her all that I had lost with this stroke and what little I had regained after about a month and a half of rehabilitation. Nothing seemed to come back with this stroke. Even though things weren't looking up for me, I told her not to be discouraged. I wasn't. After all, I had come back from previous strokes and was determined to come back from this one too. I told her to show him love, be patient and basically try to help him regain some of what he had lost by picking small tasks for him to succeed at once he was back home. The little tasks would eventually become successes and then he could move on to more difficult ones. One step at a time and she might be surprised at the outcome.

THE FROZEN YOGURT HAPPENING:

Sometimes a situation will happen that leaves you totally speechless. This is one of those situations. I developed a craving for frozen yogurt and my wife found out the hospital had a frozen yogurt stand in the cafeteria area. After checking with the nurse, she got the okay to take me down to the first floor to the yogurt stand. We purchased some. Because I was still paralyzed and in a wheel chair, she rolled me towards a table in the back of the cafeteria. We noticed there was nobody sitting in that area other than a nurse. As we passed the nurse to get seated, all of a sudden this nurse passes gas BIG TIME. It could be heard through out the cafeteria, I'm sure. My wife and I both just plain "lost it" and naturally old bucket mouth me says quite loudly, "Did you hear that?" Even though my speech was a bit slurred, the nurse heard me as well as the other folks seated in the cafeteria. The nurse calmly finished eating and left, not uttering a word, but the laughter in the cafeteria never ended. Just goes to show you that even in the midst of a crisis you can find some humor. It still makes me chuckle when I think about it.

THE RESIDENT DOCTOR OF SMALL STATURE:

Before I could be dismissed from the hospital, a young Resident Doctor was assigned to take blood from me. It was apparent that she was a small person, with a body like a midget. Now I have nothing against a person with that type of physical stature. What really bothered me was she was a doctor, and she was so small that she had to climb up on the bed and walk around me to find a suitable vein in one of my arms. The problem was every time she inserted the needle, blood spurted everywhere. By the time she finally managed to get the blood, there was blood all over the place. It was not only on the bed sheets, but also on my clothing and somehow had even managed to reach the wall next to my bed plus the ceiling. I was later told that she had been dismissed for incompetency.

THE PSYCH WARD DOCTOR:

The day prior to my discharge a doctor from the Psych Ward had been instructed to come and talk to me. He sat by my bed and said he wanted to talk and had a few questions for me which I replied "OK." He said, "Have you ever considered committing suicide?" I was dumb founded at this question. My immediate reply was in reference to what?" " The food in this hospital?" (I had found that making light of some things made my situation easier to accept.) By his reaction I could tell he really didn't appreciate my remark. His typical sterile doctor response was "Mr. Meek sometimes when a person has had numerous strokes they have a tendency to give up on life."

I had just been told that I would be going home in a wheel chair and that most likely I would never walk again. Not only was my whole left side paralyzed from my neck down but my head was also affected. It was uncontrollable and just hung on my neck like one of those weeble wobble dolls. So him asking me that question was like saying you are no longer a viable person and condemning me to a vegetable state. I point blank told him that I had no intention of giving up. It was not an option. I told him I had suffered from a major stroke previously and had recovered and was determined to do the same this time. I also told him that if I ever considered something like suicide, (which I wouldn't) my wife would help me get past such a negative thought.

While in the hospital I had a friend of many years visit. He was in charge of maintenance in his church and was a very spiritual person. Since he had read some of my writings he knew that I was also a spiritual person. He asked me if I would consider writing something for him once I was back on my feet a bit. He told me he would like a prayer. I told him I didn't know if I could do it or not because of my condition plus I was not familiar with the format of a prayer, but I would try. Although my head was completely out of wack and my left side completely paralyzed, my right hand still worked and so did my mind. So I asked my wife to bring me a pen and paper and I began to write. I would like to take time out of my story now to share with the reader what I wrote for him as well as another article while in the hospital:

IF THE ONLY WAY I CAN BE RECEIVED IN HEAVEN

Dearest Lord, I know I am not worthy of Your compassion, but I ask, if the only way I can be received into heaven is by being a stone on the pathway in, then please let my features be of a soft nature to cushion and massage your feet and the feet of those who have had a hard trip to get to your kingdom. As you walk by and if there are only clouds under your feet, please allow me to be cooling and gentle as you pass by, and if everything is not perfect with mankind, please let me be the cloth to sooth your brow or the tissue to wipe away your tears of disappointment in those who do not love you as they should. If I am a disappointment to you, then give me the strength to hold you in my heart as I should, and give me the forethought to thank you for each beautiful day and each beautiful sunset and rainbow that glorifies your doorway to heaven. Amen

As I lay in my hospital bed looking out the window, I noticed it was snowing. God once again entered into my thoughts and this is what just came out. I have no idea how, but it did.

GOD'S INFINITE WISDOM

Sometimes when winter is here and the cold winds arrive, you realize how God in His Infinite Wisdom allows a man and his mate to go outside and when the cold air blows through their clothing how two people come together to warm each other. You realize how God has allowed the cold winds to blow in the dim dreary days of winter. He allows the sunshine of their love to take away the emptiness and loneliness of winter, to be enfolded into the love of two when all else seems alone. To watch the falling of each snowflake in it's perfect features allows you to understand how a man and a woman fit together as it must have been in God's plan. It must have been in God's Infinite Wisdom to make things so much easier by making things happen for two instead of just one. And lastly to hold your loved one in the dreariness of the winter months when the sky is clear and the sounds of the birds are quiet. The house is full of happiness, and sounds of warmth just like the kitchen on a Thanksgiving morning before all the food is laid out. Now wouldn't you know that these cold bitter nights and biting winds were a definite part of God's Infinite Wisdom? So who are we to complain.

CHAPTER 6

Once I was able to leave the hospital, the doctors sent me home in a wheelchair and once again told me that most likely I would never walk again. My wife hired a nurse who checked in on me every day plus my wife would pop in all day long to see if I needed anything. Since she worked on the same property we lived at, this was no problem and worked out well. God had truly blessed me with a very special lady and a true angel which gave me a purpose to live. Since we lived in a two bedroom townhouse with two floors, it was impossible for me to sleep upstairs so my wife placed a hospital bed in our downstairs living room. Day after day I re lived my wants and desires in my mind. First I wanted to be able to walk again. I wanted to be able to open the door for my wife as I had in the past. I wanted to be able to wrap my arms around her and hug her and maybe it was selfish but I wanted to be able to go upstairs and sleep in bed with my wife.

Of course many of these wants were unrealistic in my present state but I just couldn't give up those wants and desires. They became an obsession. I had been a viable person when we married and I felt like my health issues had cheated her out of a real husband. I knew there was much I had to recover from. Truthfully at that time I didn't know if it was possible or not. Nearly everyone was telling me it simply wasn't possible but down deep I knew I couldn't give up. I would NEVER give up. After several months at home, something strange happened.

One morning before my wife left for work, she moved my wheel chair in front of the TV. I just basically sat there as game show after game show came on. I was like a weeble wobble toy. If I tried to move my head to the right, my head rolled that way and to the left the same. I eventually heard some music I recognized and suddenly realized I was moving my right foot in a slight tapping movement. I was shocked to say the least! There had been no physical changes from the weekly therapies at all. The doctors said that if there was to be a change I would know it when I felt it. Now I am a trained doctor-just a simple man who has lived through a few strokes and learned from my own physical negatives. When the change happened, nobody knew what it was or wasn't until later. I realized that for me to be able to walk again, I had to choose small goals if I was to have any chance of succeeding. A major goal would not be possible due to all I had lost.

My first goal was to start tapping my foot to a beat of music not just the right foot but the left one also. So…. day after day I would sit in the wheelchair in front of the

TV waiting for music to come on. My right foot seemed to work fairly well but the left just plain wouldn't move no matter how hard I tried. After a few weeks, I noticed a small amount of movement in my left foot. The following day it happened again. Yahoo! Two successes, first my right foot and now my left. Yes! I was on my way. Still nothing major, but I knew I was getting closer to my main goal of walking again. Although the tapping motion was becoming more frequent and becoming a little stronger, I still had a hard time sitting up and holding my head up right. My wife put pillows on both sides of my head to keep it erect, but my control was as if I was a wobbling punching bag. If I became uncomfortable and tried to turn my head it would just roll either to the left or right.

After a number of weeks of frustration, some control came back but not enough. It was time for me to consider a more intense therapy. To just sit and maintain holding my head up or to be able to turn my head to the right or left was a very slow learning process but I was determined not to give up. A funny story happened at this point in my life. My wife had come home from work and sat down on the couch where I was laying and began sewing a quilt together. (She did this in her spare time, though there wasn't much of it between painting all day and caring for me.) She had already cut the pieces out from our personal clothing. I was sleeping and after several hours had passed, I awoke and rolled to one side to find out she had actually sewed me into the quilt. We both burst into a laughing fit.

Well on with my story. Eventually I could hold my head up better and had stronger movement in my right foot but the left foot was still paralyzed with just a slight toe movement. I realized that if I did not do something, I would never see the other rooms in our townhouse again, so my next attempt was to figure out how to get around our townhouse even though I could not walk.

I attempted my own therapy, by lowering myself to the floor from my wheelchair with my right hand and arm. My left arm was totally paralyzed and I carried it close to my waist and due to lack of circulation and oxygen, it began to change into a gray whitish clammy color. My breathing capacity was poor due to partial impairment of my diaphragm from the stroke and I knew this added problem would make things much more difficult. Day after day and inch by inch I made very little progress, but I was determined. I would not give up! No way.

Every day after my wife left for work, I would tumble out of the wheelchair as if an infant and grasp the carpet and pull or crawl as far as I could. Each day I made it a little farther until I could finally reach the kitchen. When I finally accomplished this goal by pulling myself across the floor with my right arm day after day, month after month, I spotted the counter top. I realized I could reach the counter top and slowly tried to pull myself up. Once I accomplished this task, I just stood there for a few moments amazed at what I had done. I glanced down at the block floor tiles and an idea came to mind. Then suddenly another idea came to mind. Wow! I was making progress. Even though it was only a little, it was still progress. I lowered myself to the floor and crawled back to the living room to my wheelchair and waited for my wife to come home.

My wife had placed railings on both sides of our stairs when I had come home from the hospital in the hopes that one day if I regained my walking abilities and the use of my left arm, it would make it easier for me to climb the stairs. Even knowing at the time that it might never happen, she was still optimistic that one day it would. This particular morning after she left for work, I wheeled my wheelchair over to the railing. I lifted myself out of the wheelchair with my right arm and just grasped the railing. (Keep in mind even this little task took the wind right out of me). Day after day I did this and realized I was beginning to regain some balance. It took many days until one day I felt at ease standing not grasping the railing. I had succeeded! Not graceful by any means but I had succeeded. After completing this difficult task, the next step was to try to make my legs move.

I waited until my wife went to work the next morning and wheeled my wheelchair out to the kitchen area. I quickly noticed that the counter top was too far out of reach for me to grab onto so once again I tumbled out of the wheelchair and crawled to the area where the counter top was so I could pull myself up. I pulled myself up and just stood there for a few moments. I kept looking down at the tile floor. I picked out a foot square of tile then attempted to move my right leg and foot one step at a time. While doing this I tried to point my toe to the corner of the tile. I then used the heel of the right foot to point at the right and left side of the tile. I would then take my right arm and place it under my left thigh to lift my left leg up to move it and set it in place, (since it was immoveable, I realized this was the ONLY way I could get it to move.) Moving the right leg was hard to do and lifting my left leg to place it was even harder. "Oh My God", I thought, "Am I crazy, can I really do this?" My legs were stiff and it was hard to get them to function. It was extremely difficult and frustrating but I was determined not to give up. I was going to do this or die trying. I'm not really sure how many months it took but I kept at it day after day and week after week.

I did not tell or show my wife any of my progress because I was not sure it would lead to anything and I didn't want to disappoint her or myself. After a few months I could actually walk that line in the tile. My right leg worked well, but the left leg just sort of drug across the floor. Eventually I found I could lift the left leg from my hip which I had not been able to do before. I would place it, then stop. Take a step with the right foot, lift the leg, stop, take a step with the right foot, stop. I was really walking. Not perfect of course but I was walking!!! Yay.

At last a chance to show my wife. I waited that day until she came home and I reached for the door knob before she had a chance to reach it and actually opened the door for her. Later that day, after explaining what and how I had reached that point I asked her to come near me and actually got to put my arm around her and hold her. This was a major success, not to mention the fact that I was able to walk to some small degree.

My next attempt was to try to go upstairs. My wife and the nurse helped me maintain my balance the first few attempts. The first few times it took me nearly 3 hours to get up the stairs. Although each day I got better physically at walking, there were many days I was tired beyond tired, but I knew giving up was not an option. Just one step after another day after day. I was determined no matter how long it took. I was going to do this!

I truly believe that the Lord gave me the strength and perseverance to get through the struggle to recover as well as I did. My family doctor believes my walking again is a miracle. Normally if a stroke patient does not recover his or her lost mobility within 36 hours it just doesn't happen.

I knew nothing about strokes other than what we had been told by the doctors. Later on, we found out most of what the doctors had told us was the same thing found in the Medical books. It shortly became apparent that most or none of them had ever had a stroke. Because I had lived through three of them, I decided to start writing my story, hoping it would help others who have suffered from a stroke. You are reading it right now. I hope you will continue to read on.

I worked on my story day in and day out. It was a long hard process since I could only type with one hand but I continued on. As I worked on my story, an idea came to mind to write an article called "Giving Up Is Not An Option." One of our neighbors was a nurse and she stopped by one day while I was reviewing my article. In conversation, I explained to her what I was trying to do and she asked me to give her a copy of the article. Of course I did just that. Eventually she called me and asked if I would come to the hospital and speak to the Stroke Recovery Group. I agreed to do so. The day I was to speak, I arrived early and was reviewing my notes as the director came in. He started by saying "Ladies and gentleman, this is Hazen Meek, the man that wrote the stroke article." I was surprised because I had no idea that anyone other than the nurse had read my article. (You have been reading the contents of that article in this book.)

After I finished speaking to the group, I asked if there were any questions. A lady who had suffered a serious stroke said she wanted to spend some time in her garden planting and digging again but had no idea how to begin to accomplish this feat. I pondered the question for a short time and then asked her a few questions. The first question was "Do you have someone who can help you get down to your garden and will stay with you until you are ready to come back to the house?" My next question was, "Do you have someone who can get your tools for you?" I told her, "If your answer is yes to both these questions, then have someone take your tools down to your garden and then have them help you to your garden. Once you are down there, get your tools out and start digging and planting." I also told her to set a time limit so as not to over do it in the sun. I suggested she work at it every day a little at a time at first to build her strength up. I said " Before you know it, your happiness will be fulfilled and your garden will be yours again." The last time I heard, she had one of the most beautiful gardens in the area and was no longer stuck in the house. She had taken my advice and had expanded it beyond her wildest dreams.

A few years after my "recovery" as I like to call it, my wife and I also decided to join a Bowling League. Since joining the bowling league was somewhat a success, I decided to join the dart ball game group at our church. After all—my right hand worked fine and I was right handed. I could surely throw a dart and I thought it would be fun. I was excited to find something else fun to do. I soon found out how cruel some people can be. Shortly after I started, I decided to stop because some people were paying more attention to me than to the game. That Sunday after church service, one of the members asked if I was going to come to the game on Tuesday. I said "Yes, I'm thinking about it." He advised me to call the director first, rather than just showing up, so I did. I asked the director what he thought about me coming in on Tuesday to play in the game and he said, "I was glad that you stopped playing last week. Although personally I would not keep anyone from playing, its best if you do not come." I already felt like half a man and felt that was a cruel and unthoughtful thing for him to say.

In my life I have met some people who believe that everything should be perfect, but you know I have looked all over and I still haven't found a guarantee for our bodies to remain perfect. All I know is to treat it with the proper respect and take care of it. After all, you do not get a new one and even if you do have an operation to replace a defective part, it doesn't mean your body will accept it. You must take care of what you have.

Not everything I wish to try is possible but trying brings me back to being an active human being and it allows me to be able to laugh at myself. It is a true reality check and makes it easier to say "Why Not?" Instead of just "Why?"

Things seemed to be going well. WELL you say? Yes, in my opinion things were going as well as they could be, considering my circumstances.

As luck would have it, one evening my sinus's were giving me problems. I got up in the night to use the restroom and everything seemed fine, then all of a sudden I became dizzy and passed out. I awoke in my wife's arms and saw blood all over the hall. I had broken my nose in two places so off I went again to the hospital. They kept me a few days until they were sure my nose was okay. They discovered that one of my blood pressure medications had failed to function correctly which caused me to pass out. I was then sent to an eye ear nose and throat specialist who discovered a wart on the back of the nasal cavity. He removed it and did a biopsy. No cancer thank goodness. He stuffed my nose with gauze and set me up with an appointment the next day to have the gauze removed. When entering the doctor's office, she noticed my coloring was bad and stopped me and made me sit down. She took my blood pressure and said, "Oh this is too high." She decided to take it again and said "Oh no, now it is way too low." She instructed her receptionist to dial 911. Yes, you guessed it! I was rushed off to the hospital AGAIN!

I awoke in the hospital with a team of cardiac doctors surrounding me. One of the doctors said we have good news and bad news. The good news is we did an Angiogram and you have a good strong heart. The bad news is that you have suffered a minor heart attack.

My heart attack turned out to be four blockages. All about 90 per cent. They did open heart surgery. A few weeks after I was discharged, I was feeling pretty good so my wife and I decided to attend church that Sunday. Well, needless to say I passed out in church. I was rushed to the hospital by ambulance. A few days later they sent me home with a heart monitor. The day after I was placed on the heart monitor, the doctor called and asked how I was doing. I told him, "Okay." He said the heart monitor showed a drop in my pulse rate the previous night. He also said there was a good possibility that due to the descending heart rate, I might go to sleep and not wake up. He said all signs pointed to a pacemaker. He said he was preparing a room for me and for me to come to the hospital again. The following morning, they put in a pacemaker. The pacemaker did wonders. Since it redirected the oxygen to those organs that apparently were not getting enough, it also gave me back some control of my diaphragm. I was breathing better.

About two weeks after this surgery, I had so much energy I didn't know what to do with it all. My wife equated me to the Energizer Bunny. She said it was like I was on a sugar high. Of course my wife discussed this with my doctor and he informed her that I still had to be careful and not over do it. Though it was hard to corral all that energy, I tried. I certainly didn't want to have another heart attack.

We had been attending church on a regular basis again after the pace maker was implanted and everything seemed to be coming along fine for a few years.. Both our spirits were good. Things seemed to be on an up swing finally! No major incidents for awhile. It was good.. God was good!

This particular Sunday morning, the sanctuary was cool and comfortable but after the first few hymns, I started perspiring so my wife got me a tissue. I used the tissue to dry my forehead, then realized I needed to use the restroom. By the time I reached the aisle I had almost passed out. I remember 4 or 5 men coming to my aid and they and my wife trying to hold me up. The next thing I remember was sitting in a wheel chair and being transferred to a gurney and being placed in the EMT vehicle. As they loaded me into the EMT vehicle, I watched as my wife got into a friends car to follow me to the hospital. Oh my dear beloved wife whom I loved more than life itself!. I realized then how much I would miss her smile and those loving eyes, that I might never see her again. Was this it? Was this going to bet he last time I would every see her lovely face? I admit, I was scared. The tears flowed like a river down my cheeks as an EMT doctor placed an IV in my left wrist. This was the arm that was totally paralyzed since my last stroke.

I spent that Sunday and Monday in the hospital. The doctor came in late Monday afternoon and told me he had gotten the results of the cardiac echo test and all was fine and that I could go home. My wife and I were really worn out due to this ordeal so we decided to lay down for a short rest. I will never forget this day. It was August 15, 2012. It is burned in my memory. In my heart I truly believe I experienced a miracle.

I awoke after about an hour to find I had my wife's hand in mine. You are probably thinking, "Well, that isn't anything unusual." However, in this case it truly was, because her hand was resting in my left hand and I could actually feel the warmth of her hand. I noticed the dark coloring in that hand had been replaced with a warm pink color along with the return of color to my fingernails. Keep in mind, my left arm and hand had been totally paralyzed for 15 years. I had felt NOTHING in that hand. It had no movement plus the color had gone from white to a dull gray and my finger nails had turned gray also. That evening my wife put out the trash receptacles for trash pick up which was the next day then we went to bed. In the morning I got up and went out to pick up the empty containers as I usually did. (Note: since they were empty I had never had a problem picking them up with my right hand.) As I reached the garage, I looked down and noticed that I had used BOTH hands to carry the containers. I was beside myself with excitement. An idea came to mind as I looked at the debris on the garage floor. I began sweeping the area around the garage and discovered I could use both hands doing this chore also.

I was so excited. This was unbelievable. I immediately called my doctor to set up an appointment to see what, if anything was happening to my left arm and hand. It was so strange. The doctor checked me out and said he had no explanation for it. We both just looked at one another questionably and pointed up towards Heaven. He nodded his head. Even though therapy had not helped before, the doctor suggested I try it again.

Thoughts began racing through my mind at this point. This truly had to be a miracle from God. I remembered back to when I lay in the hospital bed and tried to pray the Lord's Prayer. I remember thinking what a joke this must be to God cause I couldn't even remember the words. Then I thought of all the times I had prayed to God to help me get through each ordeal and I truly believe He has given me the strength and will to keep going. But then I thought how foolish of me to think I was something special to God. Yet, I was alive. I remembered how I had learned to type with one hand. I was enjoying each new sunrise with my loving wife. I had made new friends whom I would never have met, except for the strokes. I had developed a better relationship with my brothers and sister, not to mention all the many other blessings that had crossed my path since my strokes and heart attack. Yes, I really thought I knew God., but did I really? " Why had I been spared?" I asked myself. Maybe I was spared to change things in my life or to help others. If this was God's will, I was sure I would know it in God's own time. My thoughts once again returned to the Lord's Prayer and I thought of this part of the prayer: "Thy will be done on earth as it is in heaven." I know deep inside that regardless of what lies ahead in my future, whatever happens will be God's will if it is to be so.

Shortly after my heart attack, I was diagnosed with Prostrate Cancer. I now had another major fear to contend with. I knew I was in for another long hard journey and under no circumstances could I let fear take over. Even though I had no idea what the future would hold, I told myself once again, it is in God's hands and that giving up is not an option. After this diagnosis, I do not know why, but the following incident from my childhood came to mind:

Across the street from our house was a man who did odd jobs for my mother after my dad passed away. At the end of the week he would stop by to be paid and then head for the bar to get drunk. Since he has two living sisters and I choose not to reveal his real name, I will call him Mr. Jones. Now Mr. Jones was usually OK during the day, but after a few whiskeys on Friday or Saturday night at the bar, he would shout obscenities all night long. One day I noticed him in the yard and went over to chat with him. He had a set of marble steps up to the front of his yard and there was a short tree next to them. It had a horseshoe hanging on one of the branches and every time I went by, I would wiggle it but it was always tight and did not fall. I asked him about it and he said " That horseshoe has been there as long as I have lived here and it will not come out of the tree until I pass away." A few years later, after an unusually peaceful and quiet evening the night before, I awoke the next day and had an uneasy feeling. Around noon, I told my mom I was going to go check on Mr. Jones. I walked up the steps and touched the horse shoe as I always did and it fell out of the tree at my feet. Remembering what Mr. Jones had previously told me, I ran to the front door and knocked loudly. No answer. No sound from within. I walked around the side porch and tried peeking in but couldn't see a thing, but. I did hear a strange sound like thousands of buzzing flies. I looked up and the window was covered with them. I ran to my neighbors home and told them to call the police. When the police went in, they found Mr. Jones lying on his living room floor. What he had told me about his horse shoe had come true. He had passed away.

I couldn't help but wonder if this was God's way of telling me what might lie ahead for me. Was this an omen? Is this to be my end? If it is, my prayer to the Lord is this: "I really hate to ask but could you please help me one more time? Regardless of the outcome, I want to thank you again for each beautiful day of my life. Amen."

Other articles I have written:

(Written for my wife)

A LADY

How does one recognize a lady? First of all she will listen to your remarks without being condescending. If she disagrees she will then ask you further as to your remarks. She will allow you to either bury yourself deeper or re-track your misstatement. She normally will not take your remarks as offensive unless they are vulgar. In fact vulgarity will not be tolerated and she will call you on the remarks. She may even ask you: Do you speak that same language in front of your mother?. If she sees the chip on your shoulder, she will knock it off in a real lady like way. She will not use her fists but in a unique way, leaving you in a state of confusion and sometimes not knowing what she just did. My wife has a look that is truly powerful in its own way, and more powerful than a switch - that look will take your feet out from underneath your body. It will leave you off balance and speechless for an undetermined amount of time. Never think you are not in front of a lady for they will mask it well. I thank God I am lucky enough to be married to one.

MOTHER EARTH WHO?

She sees you in the morning.
She sees you when you rise.

Looks on from stagnant shadows,
With her scarlet eyes.

As she looks across the littered highway,
It almost brings her to her knees.

With children having children
And birth control a breeze.

Lets build a few more houses
And cut down a few more trees.

And the odors most foul and pungent brings tears
into her eyes,
As she puts on her happiest of faces as the brown
factory smoke sears the morning skies.

It's no secret her heart is breaking and the green
foliage is burning up,
There's a rumble from her belly as time is coming
surely. In fact, she's almost done.

As we feel the quake within her heart, for it's
mother earth who's leaving as truth comes to pass.
Now these signs are clear and obvious as dew upon
the grass.

Just take the time to pick up the waste scattered
across her land,
Or bits of off shore drilling that soaked within her
sands.

Shake hands with your closest neighbors and surely
make a pact.
Before her death most obvious, before her heart does
crack.

Her land is oh so precious and it is left to you and I,
For it is God's gift, this precious orb floating in
the sky.

Let's begin our step backwards in a more
intelligent way,
And save our precious earth. In fact, let's you and I
begin today!

They say it only takes one to make a decision to impact
the earth to face another day. As our universe is calling,
let's help mother earth in her universal balance as she plays
among the stars. For earth is but a diamond who's been
polished and shines within the sky. Put down the chiseling
hammer and pick up the polishing cloth. Brighten up her
luster to be an example to others across the vastness of space,
to show what we have done to protect our human race.
Mother earth is just a metaphor for what we should really
do to protect her as our loved ones did and would also want
us to.

ABOUT THIS BOOK
AND ITS AUTHORS

(compiled by a friend)

First, let me say that I have chosen to remain anonymous since all I did was compile Hazen and Linda's story for them. The real credit goes to them for the story is written in their own words. You have just finished reading what they lived through for 19 years. It is a true story and was written from the depths of their hearts.

Now I would like to explain to the reader how the writing of their story came about....

HAZEN:

After his third stroke, Hazen was in the hospital undergoing therapy for a number of months. During his stay in the hospital he came into contact with other stroke patients. Many of these individuals were discouraged and depressed over the dilemma they suddenly found themselves in. Of course he had his bad days too, but even so, he continually tried to encourage them not to give up. After all, this was his third stroke. He'd been through it twice before. He had worked diligently during his first two strokes with physical therapists and rehabilitation technicians to recover. Once released from the hospital he then decided to continue therapy on his own and had recovered fairly well. But this time was different. This stroke was quite severe. Things didn't look good and he knew that. Many times, he felt just as discouraged as those persons he had met, but he never let on that this was how he felt inside. He always had a smile for every one who crossed his path. (though his smile was a bit crooked, it was still a smile) and he would ask how "they" were doing. That was Hazen! Even though he was in a wheel chair, had little control of his head, his speech slurred, and paralyzed, day after day, he continued to smile to all he met and encourage them to hang in there and never give up.

After months of physical therapy plus months of struggling with his own personal therapy after returning home, a neighbor who happened to be a nurse, observed how much he had accomplished. She was highly impressed with how far he had come. Eventually she approached him and asked him to give a speech to the stroke recovery group in the hospital where she worked. He agreed to do so. He wrote a short speech outlining his experience and struggles to recover. He then presented his speech to the stroke patient group at the hospital as promised. He chose the title "Giving Up is Not an Option" for his speech.

Hazen was a very compassionate man with a burning

desire to help others facing similar struggles as his own. He wanted to help as many people as possible, so he decided to turn his speech into a book and have it published. He would sit at the computer day after day, for years typing out his own personal experiences and thoughts as they came to mind. He continued to revise these thoughts and experiences through the years. This was an extremely difficult task for him since he could only type with one hand. (I can now truly appreciate how very hard this was for him, because while in the process of compiling his and Linda's story, I broke my left arm. I tried to continue compiling their story by typing with one hand and believe me, it is EXTREMELY difficult, if not impossible.) I finally gave up due to the difficulty and laid it aside until my arm became functional again. How ironic!. And to think the title of his book is "Giving Up is Not An Option"

LINDA:

When Hazen became bedridden with prostrate cancer, Linda also began writing down her feelings and thoughts concerning their relationship and his illness. As you may have noticed, her thoughts and his vary a bit when speaking about some of the same situations. Keep in mind each saw it from their own personal perspective as they remembered it .

In her heart she really believed he was going to be okay. After all… they had been through three strokes, and a major heart attack together, but unfortunately this time it wasn't meant to be. For months she tended to his every need. Some nights going without sleep just to be at his beckon call should he need anything. Such devotion these days is rare but then their love for each other was also rare indeed. They shared a love that most people can only dream about. They shared a bond so solid that even death could not break it. As you have learned by reading the prologue, (written by her) Hazen passed away from the prostrate cancer on March 15, 2013.

After Hazen passed away, Linda was going through some of his writings on the computer and found this note to her: " My dearest Linda, If I do not make it please make sure my manuscript gets published. It has so much to do with us. I love you! It will help others. All I ever wanted was your complete love and that gave me reason to live. My heart has reached it's point of decision and the medication is not working and as hard as I have tried to explain to you, you cannot seem to understand."

He knew his time on this earth was coming to a close as he wrote this. His last thoughts were of Linda and helping others. Linda had always known how badly Hazen wanted his work published and finding this note on the computer confirmed it even more.

Shortly after discovering what he had written, she called me to let me know what she had found on the computer. She was so overcome with grief that she kept bursting into tears each time we started to discuss it. It was all so overwhelming for her. Eventually as things began to got a little easier for her, we agreed to work together to fulfill Hazen's wishes. Although it has taken us nearly a year, we have finally accomplished what in his heart he had truly wanted all those years. And so now you know how the story you just read came to be.

Rest in Peace Hazen…. It is done!

us in our first apartment after we were married, 1983.

hazen's graduation from computer school, less than
a year after his third stroke. he came in second in
his class and perfect attendance. he would get up at
3am to study. notice the clenched left hand, he had
that for the rest of his life, but worked around it.

hazen in our candle shop, 1984, right after we were married.
we loved working together and meeting folks. he liked to talk
to everyone if they didn't buy anything or not. a born talker.

hazen with dakota, 1992 on vacation before any strokes.

Lightning Source UK Ltd.
Milton Keynes UK
UKOW04f1204220215

246622UK00001B/25/P